FOREX TRADING

WITH PYTHON

MADE EASY

(The Python Forex Trader's Handbook)

Unleash the Python Power for Turning Data into Gold in Forex Markets

James Vega

TABLE OF CONTENT

Chapter One

    Introduction to Algorithmic Forex Trading

        Entering the Realm of Automated Currency Exchange

        Why Python? Unleashing the Serpent's Power

        Navigating the Vast Forex Sea

        Demystifying the Bots: Automation in Action

Chapter Two

    Python Programming Basics

        Setting Up Your Python Environment

        Essential Data Structures and Functions

        Control Flow and Error Handling

Chapter Three

    Financial Data Acquisition and Manipulation

        Unleashing the Power of Data in Forex Trading

        Accessing Forex Market Data using Python Libraries

        Cleaning, Organizing, and Manipulating Financial Data

        Time Series Analysis and Building DataFrames

Chapter Four

    Technical Analysis Using Python

        Unleashing the Power of Python for Chart Insights

        Popular Technical Indicators and Their Python Implementations

        Backtesting Indicators and Strategies using

Python

Python Libraries for Backtesting:

Chapter Five

Quantitative Analysis and Modeling

Chapter Six

Machine Learning for Algorithmic Trading

Supervised vs. Unsupervised Learning:

Building and Optimizing Trading Models:

Chapter Seven

Designing Your Trading Strategy

Defining Entry and Exit Points using Python Code

Entry Strategies:

Risk Management and Position-Sizing Strategies

Optimizing Your Strategy via Backtesting and Simulation

Chapter Eight

Building Your Trading Bot Using Python

Connecting to a Forex Broker API using Python

Implementing Your Trading Strategy in Python Code

Testing and Debugging Your Trading Bot

Chapter Nine

Deployment and Live Trading - Taking the Plunge

Considerations for Live Trading:

Chapter Ten

Algorithmic Trading Platforms and Tools

Integrating Your Python Bot

Chapter Eleven

4

Backtesting and Optimization Techniques

Master the Algorithmic Forge

Performance Metrics Beyond the Basics:

Chapter Twelve

The Future of Algorithmic Trading

Emerging Trends and Technologies:

Ethical Considerations and Responsible Trading
Practices:

Conclusion:

Epilogue

Your Algorithmic Trading Journey

Final Tips for Algorithmic Triumph:

Appendix

Sample Python Code for Basic Trading
Strategies

Part One:
Foundations of
Algorithmic Trading

Chapter One

Introduction to Algorithmic Forex Trading

Entering the Realm of Automated Currency Exchange

Because of technological advancements, the boundaries between human intuition and the accuracy of algorithms have become more blurry in the world of finance, which has experienced a revolution. Python is a language that has emerged as a formidable tool for people who are looking to traverse the dynamic foreign exchange market. This language is used in the field of algorithmic trading.

Why Python? Unleashing the Serpent's Power

Python emerges as a favorite option among traders for various convincing reasons:

Readability and Simplicity: Python's syntax matches normal language, making it simple to learn and grasp, especially for individuals without strong coding backgrounds. This clarity speeds the learning curve and facilitates the creation of trading techniques.

Effective Libraries Python is home to a vast ecosystem of libraries that have been developed with the express purpose of facilitating financial research and trading. These libraries include:

- Numpy for Numerical computations.
- pandas for data processing and analysis

- Matplotlib and Seaborn For data visualization.
- The TA-Lib for technical analysis indicators.
- Backtrader for backtesting trading strategies

Open-Source and Active Community: Python's open-source nature encourages a thriving community of developers who regularly contribute to its libraries and resources. This united effort guarantees access to cutting-edge technologies and information exchange.

Cross-Platform Compatibility: Python effortlessly operates across Windows, macOS, and Linux, enabling flexibility in your trading environment.

Challenges to Embrace:

While Python provides many benefits, it's vital to identify possible challenges:

- **Performance Optimization**: For high-frequency trading, Python could need optimization methods to match the performance of lower-level languages like C++.

- **grasp Curve**: While somewhat beginner-friendly, Python nevertheless demands devotion to grasp its syntax and resources properly.

Navigating the Vast Forex Sea

The Forex market, or foreign exchange market, ranks as the world's biggest and most liquid financial market. It centers on the exchange of currencies, driven by global commerce, investment, and speculation. Key aspects of the Forex market include:

- 24/7 Operation: Trading happens around the clock, covering various time zones.
- High Liquidity: The huge number of transactions promotes quick order execution and tight spreads.
- Volatility: Currency values vary frequently, affected by economic events, political changes, and market opinion.
- Leverage: Forex brokers sometimes provide leverage, enabling traders to hold greater positions with a lower initial deposit. However, leverage multiplies both earnings and losses.

Demystifying the Bots: Automation in Action

Trading bots, also known as algorithmic trading systems, automate the decision-making process, executing transactions based on specified rules and algorithms. They provide various advantages:

- Emotionless Trading: Bots avoid the psychological biases that frequently impair human traders, following solely the programmed approach.
- Enhanced Efficiency: Bots may monitor several markets and execute deals fast, seizing on opportunities that could be overlooked by traditional traders.
- Backtesting Capabilities: Bots allow the testing of trading methods on past data to

estimate their prospective performance before risking actual cash.

By utilizing the power of Python, traders can construct sophisticated trading bots, analyze massive volumes of market data, and apply complicated trading strategies with accuracy.

This chapter has provided the framework for our journey into the intriguing realm of algorithmic Forex trading. Prepare to embark on a trip that merges financial experience with the beauty of Python coding, navigating the turbulent Forex market with increased clarity and control.

Chapter Two

Python Programming Basics

Welcome to Python, your path to algorithmic Forex trading! In this chapter, we'll establish the basis for your Python adventure, leading you through:

- Setting up your Python environment: Get everything you need to start coding effortlessly.
- Essential data structures and functions: Learn the basic blocks of Python coding.
- Control flow and error handling: Make your programs make choices and handle glitches gracefully.

Ready to dig in? Let's go!

Setting Up Your Python Environment

Installing Python:

- Download the current version from https://www.python.org/downloads/
- Follow the installation instructions for your operating system.

Choosing an IDE or Text Editor:

IDEs (Integrated Development Environments) provide capabilities like code completion and debugging. Popular choices include:

- PyCharm
- Visual Studio Code
- Thonny (excellent for novices)
- Text editors like Sublime Text or Notepad++ are simpler but give less instruction.

Essential Data Structures and Functions

- Variables: Containers for holding data, such as numbers, text, or lists.
- Data Types: Specify what sort of data a variable contains (e.g., integers, floats, texts).
- Operators: Perform calculations and comparisons (e.g., +, -, *, /, ==, !=, >, <).
- Functions: Reusable chunks of code that execute certain functions.
- Control Flow Statements: Control the sequence in which code is executed (e.g., if, else, for, while).

Control Flow and Error Handling

- Conditional Statements (if, Elif, else): Make judgments based on circumstances.

- Loops (for, while): Repeat code blocks numerous times.
- Error Handling (attempt, except): Prevent crashes and handle errors graciously.

Practice Makes Perfect

Interact with Python directly in your environment to explore these topics.

Stay tuned! In the following chapter, we'll dig into financial data collecting and modification, giving you the ability to handle Forex market data using Python.

Chapter Three

Financial Data Acquisition and Manipulation

Unleashing the Power of Data in Forex Trading

"In God we trust, all others must bring data." – W. Edwards Deming

In the realm of algorithmic trading, data is the gasoline that propels your tactics. This chapter offers you the skills and procedures to successfully obtain, clean, organize, and analyze financial data, setting the foundation for constructing lucrative trading algorithms.

Accessing Forex Market Data using Python Libraries

Opening the Data Gateways: Explore typical data sources for Forex market data, including:

- Free sources: Yahoo Finance, Quandl, Alpha Vantage
- Paid providers: OANDA, FXCM, Interactive Brokers

Understand the subtleties of multiple data formats (CSV, JSON, API)

Wielding the Right Tools for the Job: Master Python libraries necessary for data acquisition:

- pandas: The powerhouse for data processing and analysis
- requests: Fetching data from web sources

- yfinance: Streamlined access to Yahoo Finance data
- quandl: Interface for accessing Quandl's financial datasets
- fix-python: Interacting with FIX (Financial Information eXchange) protocol

Retrieving Data using Python Code:

- Walk through hands-on examples of getting Forex data using each library
- Parse and extract essential information from multiple data types
- Handle probable errors and exceptions gently

Cleaning, Organizing, and Manipulating Financial Data

Taming the Data Beast:

Address typical data quality issues:

- Missing values
- Outliers
- Inconsistent formatting

Employ cleaning procedures like:

- Filling missing data using suitable techniques (mean, median, interpolation)
- Identifying and treating outliers using statistical approaches
- Reformatting data for consistency

Shaping Data to Your Will:

- Master strategies for organizing and rearranging data:

- Selecting particular columns and rows
- Resampling data to various time frequencies (daily, hourly, etc.)
- Creating new computed columns (e.g., moving averages, volatility measures)
- Leverage pandas' strong data wrangling capabilities

Time Series Analysis and Building DataFrames

Unveiling Patterns in Time:

- Understand the notion of time series data and its usefulness in Forex trading

Explore approaches for time series analysis:

- Visualizing trends and patterns using plots (line charts, candlestick charts)

- Calculating basic statistics (mean, standard deviation, volatility)
- Decomposing time series into trend, seasonality, and noise components

Constructing Data Fortresses:
- Build powerful pandas DataFrames to store and manipulate financial data
- Handle time-based activities effectively
- Create meaningful infographics to expose hidden truths

Ready, Set, Analyze!

With a strong foundation in data collecting and manipulation, you're now able to begin on the thrilling path of Forex data exploration and analysis. The following chapters will expand upon these abilities, taking you through technical analysis, quantitative modeling, and machine learning approaches to find successful trading opportunities in the Forex market.

Part Two: Building Your Trading Toolbox

Chapter Four

Technical Analysis Using Python

Unleashing the Power of Python for Chart Insights

Technical analysis (TA) serves as a cornerstone for many forex traders. By examining previous price patterns and indication signs, traders try to forecast future market movements and make educated trading choices. In this chapter, we'll go into the area of TA using Python, equipping you to:

- Calculate and display common technical indicators
- Backtest their performance using previous data

- Create bespoke indicators customized to your particular approach

Popular Technical Indicators and Their Python Implementations

Let's study a few crucial technical indicators and their Python implementations utilizing popular libraries like pandas_ta and TA-Lib:

Moving Averages (MA)

Smooth out price volatility and emphasize trends

- Simple Moving Average (SMA): pandas_ta.sma(df['Close'], length=20)
- Exponential Moving Average (EMA): pandas_ta.ema(df['Close'], length=20)
- Relative Strength Index (RSI)

- Measures momentum and overbought/oversold levels
- pandas_ta.rsi(df['Close'], length=14)

Bollinger Bands

- Define volatility bands around price

pandas_ta.bbands(df['Close'], length=20, std=2)

- Moving Average Convergence Divergence (MACD)

- Identifies trend changes and momentum shifts

pandas_ta.macd(df['Close'], fast=12, slow=26, signal=9)

Python Code Examples for Indicator Calculation:

```python
Python

import pandas as pd

import pandas_ta as ta


# Load example Forex data

df = pd.read_csv('EURUSD_data.csv')


# Calculate indicators

df.ta.rsi(close='Close', length=14) # Calculate RSI

df.ta.bbands(close='Close', length=20, std=2) # Calculate Bollinger Bands
```

Backtesting Indicators and Strategies using Python

Backtesting is vital for analyzing the possible performance of indicators and strategies before risking actual cash. Here's a simple backtesting technique using Python:

- Load historical data: Fetch historical Forex data for your preferred currency pair.
- Define trading rules: Set particular entry and exit criteria depending on indicator indications.
- Simulate trades: Iterate over historical data, using trading rules to create hypothetical buy and sell signals.
- Track performance: Calculate measures including total return, win rate,

risk-reward ratio, and drawdowns to analyze strategy success.

Python Libraries for Backtesting:

- backtrader: Framework for creating and backtesting trading strategies
- zipline: Backtesting and live trading platform

Customizing Indicators and Building Your Own

The fundamental strength of Python rests in its flexibility. You may construct custom indicators to fit your trading style and market circumstances. Here's a simple framework:

- Define the indicator's logic: Formulate the mathematical computations or criteria for your indicator.

31

- Write Python functions: Implement the logic using Python functions, utilizing libraries like NumPy and pandas for data processing.
- Integrate with your trading system: Apply the custom indicator to produce signals and include it in your backtesting and trading techniques.

Key Takeaways:

- Python provides a robust toolbox for technical analysis in forex trading.
- Mastering common indicators and backtesting procedures is vital for constructing efficient trading strategies.
- Custom indicators may fine-tune your strategy and perhaps find new market information.

- Continuously review and adjust your indicators and techniques depending on backtesting outcomes and market circumstances.

Chapter Five

Quantitative Analysis and Modeling

Welcome to the domain of numbers, where patterns dance across timeframes and hidden linkages whisper hints to market moves. This chapter goes into the intriguing area of quantitative analysis and modelling, arming you with strong tools to deconstruct Forex data and expose its secrets. Buckle up, Python coder, as we go on a fantastic voyage through:

1. Unveiling the Symphony of Statistics:

Statistical analysis is the core of quantitative trading. It's like a microscope, amplifying minor intricacies inside market data. Let's investigate some prominent musicians in this statistical orchestra:

- Mean: The core of the matter, the average value of a dataset. Deviations from the mean signify possible trading opportunities.

- Variance: The dance floor's size, measuring how spaced apart data points are. more variance suggests volatility, bringing more potential benefits and hazards.

- Standard Deviation: The mean's bodyguard, measuring the average distance of data points from the mean. A low standard deviation denotes stability, whereas a large one foreshadows instability.

- Correlation: The whisperer of linkages, uncovering hidden connections between distinct assets or indications. Positive correlations imply comparable motions, whereas negative ones hint at conflicting patterns.

Armed with these facts, you can:
- Identify undervalued or overpriced currencies based on mean deviations.
- Gauge volatility and adapt risk management techniques depending on the variation.
- Exploit hidden links between currencies via correlation analysis.

2. The Art of Statistical Arbitrage: Unearthing Inefficiencies

Remember the thrill of discovering $20 money on the sidewalk? Statistical arbitrage delivers precisely that pleasure, identifying mispricings in the market owing to inefficiencies. Think of it as a magician plucking rabbits out of hats, except instead of fluffy bunnies, you conjure gains from market peculiarities. Here's how:

- Cointegration: Imagine two currencies dancing in perfect sync. Cointegration recognizes such correlations, enabling you to exploit price disparities by purchasing the undervalued and selling the overpriced.

- Mean Reversion: Markets, like rollercoasters, ultimately return to normality. Mean reversion recognizes these "mean lines" and allows you to benefit from deviations by purchasing during falls and selling at peaks.

- Calendar Spreads: Seasons vary, and so do market values. Calendar spreads utilize expected seasonal price changes in connected assets, such as agricultural commodities.

By mastering these statistical arbitrage strategies, you can convert market inefficiencies into your treasure mine.

3. From Past to Future: Demystifying Time Series Forecasting

Gazing into the crystal ball of the future may be fiction, but time series forecasting in Python gets very near. It's like peeking into the market's DNA, evaluating its history to forecast its future dance moves. Let's look inside the toolbox:

- Moving Averages: These smooth out the market's pulse, exposing underlying tendencies. varied forms, such as Simple Moving Averages (SMA) and Exponential

Moving Averages (EMA), adapt to varied market circumstances.

- Autoregressive Integrated Moving Average (ARIMA): This statistical powerhouse forecasts future values based on prior data and mistakes. Think of it as a statistical time machine, anticipating future prices based on previous trends.

- Machine Learning (ML) Models: Enter the domain of artificial intelligence! Algorithms like Neural Networks and Support Vector Machines may discover intricate associations within data, enabling even more advanced predicting capabilities.

Remember: Forecasting is not crystal clear, but it's a strong tool to educate your trading tactics and forecast market developments.

Putting it all Together:

Now, imagine: You wield the scalpel of statistical analysis, analyze market data with arbitrage accuracy, and foresee future patterns with the knowledge of a time traveler. This is the power of quantitative analysis and modeling. Use these tools intelligently, backtest your methods meticulously, and remember, in the dynamic world of Forex, even the finest models require regular monitoring and adjustments.

This chapter is only the beginning of your quantitative adventure. Explore further into sophisticated statistical approaches, dig into particular ML algorithms, and remember, the most effective tool is not the model itself, but the knowledge that underlies its usage. Go out, Python coder, and conquer the Forex markets with the symphony of numbers!

Chapter Six

Machine Learning for Algorithmic Trading

The field of algorithmic trading has just taken a quantum leap. While conventional technical analysis and quantitative modeling offered strong tools, Machine Learning (ML) injects a dose of automation and pattern recognition, opening doors to previously inconceivable forecasting potential. This chapter goes into the area of ML, offering you the knowledge and abilities to maximize its potential for lucrative Forex trading.

Supervised vs. Unsupervised Learning:

Imagine strolling into a library with neatly organized books — guided learning. Each book bears a clear title (e.g., "history," "fiction"), leading your search for particular content. Similarly, supervised algorithms "learn" from labeled historical data by recognizing patterns and links between inputs (market data) and desired outputs (price forecasts, buy/sell signals). Popular methods here include Linear Regression, Support Vector Machines, and Decision Trees.

Unsupervised learning, on the other hand, is like wandering a maze bookshop — you come across intriguing connections without pre-defined categories. Unsupervised algorithms identify underlying patterns and groups within data without explicit labeling. Techniques like K-Means Clustering and Principal Component research (PCA) may uncover market abnormalities, cluster comparable price movements, and even produce synthetic financial data for additional research.

Applying ML to Forex Data:

Forex data contains a rich mine of information — prices, volumes, indications, news events, and more. Utilizing supervised learning, we can train models to:

- Predict price movements: By supplying past price data as inputs and future prices as outputs, we may train algorithms to anticipate market patterns, helping us discover probable entry and exit locations.
- Generate trading signals: Leverage algorithms to assess various data points and generate buy/sell signals based on learning patterns, automating your trading choices.

- Optimize current strategies: Enhance your technical analysis tools by feeding indicator values and price data to supervised models, improving entry/exit rules and risk management settings.

Unsupervised learning delivers equally useful insights:

- Market segmentation: Identify unique clusters of price movements, enabling you to customize trading methods to various market regimes.
- Anomaly detection: Uncover anomalous pricing patterns and probable market aberrations, helping you to forecast rapid movements or avoid potential hazards.
- Data generation: Generate synthetic Forex data approximating real-world events, enabling you to stress-test your strategies

and refine models without depending entirely on historical data.

Building and Optimizing Trading Models:

Building an ML model that reliably predicts future prices or delivers lucrative trading signals isn't magic. It's a rigorous procedure requiring numerous important steps:

- Data pre-processing: Cleaning, standardizing, and organizing your Forex data to guarantee the model gets high-quality inputs.
- Feature engineering: Transforming raw data into features (technical indicators, statistical computations) that capture valuable market information.

- Model selection: Choosing the proper method depending on your data and intended output (regression for prediction, classification for signal creation).
- Training and testing: Splitting your data into training and testing sets, using the training set to "teach" the model and the testing set to assess its performance.
- Hyperparameter tuning: Fine-tuning model parameters for best performance — finding the sweet spot between complexity and accuracy.
- Backtesting and validation: Evaluate your model's performance using historical data to determine its real-world effectiveness and uncover any shortcomings.

Remember: ML models are amazing tools, but they're not crystal balls. Always practice responsible trading, regularly check your models, and combine them with current risk management measures to traverse the volatile Forex market.

Bonus Tip: Explore cutting-edge research on utilizing Deep Learning methods, like as recurrent neural networks, to capture intricate temporal correlations in Forex data and possibly uncover even more advanced prediction models.

By embracing the potential of ML, you're not simply constructing trading bots; you're taking a major stride towards a future when data becomes your most important tool in navigating the ever-evolving Forex environment. So, dig into the intriguing realm of ML, polish your abilities, and discover the hidden possibilities inside your

Forex data. The market awaits your algorithmic brilliance!

This chapter, within the specified length of 1000 words, tries to present a quick but thorough review of Machine Learning for Algorithmic Forex Trading. Feel free to alter the amount of depth and further explore individual algorithms, code examples, and resources to improve your knowledge and construct your ML-powered trading strategies.

The adventure into the realm of algorithmic trading continues! Stay tuned for later chapters in this course to uncover the full potential of Python coding for lucrative Forex trading.

Part Three: Building and Deploying Your Forex Trading Bot

Chapter Seven

Designing Your Trading Strategy

Welcome to the core of algorithmic trading! In this chapter, we'll painstakingly build a trading strategy that corresponds with your risk tolerance, market view, and Python proficiency. We'll walk you through the complexity of identifying entry and exit points, adopting comprehensive risk management approaches, and effectively improving your strategy via backtesting and simulation.

Defining Entry and Exit Points using Python Code

Just as a great chef understands when to add ingredients and when to take a dish from the fire, a successful trader must exactly determine when to enter and quit the market. Python, our trusty kitchen companion, helps us to transform these trade choices into practical code.

Entry Strategies:

- Technical Indicators: Python's financial libraries, such as pandas and TA-Lib, provide a large selection of technical indicators to flag possible entry positions.

Utilize them to detect:
- Moving average crossings
- RSI breakouts
- MACD divergences
- Bollinger Band squeezes

Breakouts and Reversals: Code conditional statements to trigger trades when prices breach important levels or demonstrate reversal patterns.

Fundamental Analysis:

While algorithmic trading frequently depends on technical indications, Python's web scraping capabilities may combine fundamental data streams for a holistic strategy.

Exit Strategies:

Stop-Loss Orders:

Implement this critical risk management tool using Python's order placement routines to automatically quit trades when losses reach predefined amounts.

Take-Profit Orders:

Secure profits by establishing automatic exit points based on target prices or percentage gains.

Trailing Stops:

Python's dynamic computations let you trail stop-loss orders as prices move positively, safeguarding profits while providing opportunities for future gains.

Risk Management and Position-Sizing Strategies

No trading approach is failsafe. Embracing this fact and applying solid risk management procedures is vital to long-term success. Python lets you measure risk and alter position sizes appropriately.

Risk Per Trade:

Define the maximum proportion of your money you're prepared to risk on each deal.

Position Sizing:

Calculate optimal trade sizes depending on risk tolerance, stop-loss levels, and account size.

Volatility Adjustment:
Adapt position sizes dynamically depending on market volatility using Python's volatility computations.

Maximum Drawdown:
Monitor the maximum peak-to-trough decrease in your portfolio's value and adopt protections to avoid excessive losses.

Optimizing Your Strategy via Backtesting and Simulation

Before risking actual cash, go on a trip through time utilizing Python's backtesting features. Test your approach against past market data to assess its potential performance and discover areas for improvement.

Backtesting Frameworks:
Leverage Python modules like Backtrader or Zipline to simulate trades on historical data and gather performance metrics.

Performance Analysis:
Calculate critical parameters such as win rate, profit factor, Sharpe ratio, and drawdown to analyze strategy success.

Parameter Optimization:
Fine-tune strategy parameters (e.g., indicator thresholds, stop-loss levels) to optimize performance.

Walk-Forward Optimization:

Employ this approach to mimic strategy performance across diverse market situations, verifying its resilience.

Remember, Backtesting results don't guarantee future success, but they give useful insights for strategy development and risk assessment.

Designing a good trading strategy involves a combination of market understanding, risk management expertise, and Python coding abilities. By carefully identifying entry and exit points, using strong risk management concepts, and rigorously improving your approach via backtesting, you'll construct a solid basis for your algorithmic trading adventure.

Chapter Eight

Building Your Trading Bot Using Python

It's time to bring your trading plan to life using the power of Python. In this chapter, we'll lead you through the process of constructing a trading bot that can autonomously execute your well-prepared forex trading choices.

Connecting to a Forex Broker API using Python

API Selection:

Choose a Forex broker that has a Python-friendly API with good documentation and tutorials.

Consider aspects including trading costs, account minimums, provided currency pairings, and API functions.

API Authentication:

Obtain your API credentials (typically an API key and secret key) from your broker's platform. Store these credentials carefully, since they enable access to your trading account.

Installation of Necessary Libraries:

- Install the Python library for your broker's API, such as OANDApyV20 for OANDA or fxcmpy for FXCM.
- Install additional libraries for data processing and analysis, such as pandas, numpy, and requests.

Establishing the Connection:

Python
import oandapyV20
client =
oandapyV20.API(access_token="YOUR_API_TOKEN")
account_id = "YOUR_ACCOUNT_ID"
instruments = "EUR_USD"
client.request(oandapyV20.endpoints.instruments(account_id, instruments))
Use code with discretion

Implementing Your Trading Strategy in Python Code

Defining Entry and Exit Conditions:

Python
def buy_signal(data):
# Logic for identifying buy signals
return condition_is_met

def sell_signal(data):
# Logic for identifying sell signals
return condition_is_met

Executing Trades:

Python

```
function place_order(instrument, units, side,
type, price=None):

data = {

"order": {

"instrument": instrument,

"units": units,

"side": side,

"type": type,

"price": price

} }
```

return
client.request(oandapyV20.endpoints.orders(ac count_id), data)
Use code with discretion

Risk Management:

Python
def calculate_position_size(risk_percentage, account_balance, stop_loss_pips):
# Calculate position size based on risk parameters
return position_size
Use code with discretion.

Testing and Debugging Your Trading Bot

Backtesting:

Simulate your approach using historical data to assess its performance and make improvements.

Use libraries like Backtrader or zipline for efficient backtesting.

Paper Trading:

- Test your bot in a virtual environment without risking real dollars.

- Most brokers provide demo accounts, particularly for this reason.

Live Trading (with Caution):

- Start with tiny dosages and watch performance attentively.

- Implement effective risk management strategies to safeguard your money.

Debugging:

Use print statements, logging, and Python's debugging tools to find and rectify issues.
Handle exceptions gently to avoid unexpected bot crashes.

Additional Tips:

- **Modular Design**: Break down your code into functions and classes for improved structure and maintainability.
- **Clear Documentation**: Explain your code's logic and functionality for future reference and collaboration.
- **Version Control:** Use Git or other version control systems to monitor changes and revert to prior versions if required.

- **Continuous Learning**: Stay current with the newest Python libraries and best practices in algorithmic trading.

Remember, Building a successful trading bot involves a mix of programming abilities, trading experience, and risk management competence. Patience, tenacity, and continual learning are important for success in this career.

Chapter Nine

Deployment and Live Trading – Taking the Plunge

So, you've methodically constructed your Forex trading bot, a formidable Python warrior trained via rigorous backtesting and simulation. But before putting it into the real-world battlefield, remember this: live trading is a different beast, where market whims may shred even the best-laid strategies. This chapter offers you the tactical armor required to negotiate this hostile world, ensuring your bot not only lives but flourishes.

Considerations for Live Trading:

1. Risk Management is Paramount: Live trading is when theory meets reality, and reality may be severe. A single poor transaction may destroy your whole portfolio. Thus, strong risk management is non-negotiable. Here are essential strategies:

- Position Sizing: Limit your exposure to each transaction using established criteria like the Kelly Criterion or the Fixed Fraction calculation. Don't allow a single transaction to make or destroy your portfolio.

- Stop-Loss Orders: Always establish automated stop-loss orders to automatically quit a trade when losses exceed a specified level. This lowers downside risk and eliminates emotional panic selling.

- Take-Profit Orders: Define profit objectives using take-profit orders, locking in gains, and collecting profits when your strategy meets its aim. Greed may be your adversary, so be disciplined and protect your victories.

2. Prioritize Security:

The digital arena is replete with predators, therefore bot security is vital. Here's how to harden your defenses:

- Code Obfuscation: Obfuscate your bot's code to make it less legible and prone to reverse engineering. This offers a layer of protection against possible copycats.

- Secure Servers: Deploy your bot on trusted, secure servers with powerful firewalls and encryption to preserve your code and trade data.

- Two-Factor Authentication: Implement two-factor authentication for access to your trading accounts and platforms, offering an additional degree of protection against unwanted access.

3. Backtesting Revisited:

While backtesting gave significant information, the actual market is a dynamic beast. Revisit your backtesting with a critical eye:

- Stress Testing: Subject your bot to harsh market circumstances beyond your original backtesting settings. This identifies possible flaws and helps modify your approach for unanticipated turbulence.

- Out-of-Sample Testing: Test your bot on data not utilized in the first backtesting, guaranteeing its effectiveness on unseen market data. This offers a more accurate measure of live performance.

Monitoring and Optimizing Performance:

Deploying your bot is only the beginning. Live trading is a constant learning process:

- Real-time Monitoring: Closely monitor your bot's performance in real-time, monitoring its transactions, profit/loss, and critical data. Use trade dashboards and visualizations to acquire a holistic perspective.

- Performance Analysis: Regularly examine your bot's performance using measures like profit factor, Sharpe ratio, and drawdown. Identify opportunities for improvement and adjust your plan based on actual market data.

- Journaling and Reflection: Maintain a trading diary, chronicling your choices, achievements, and mistakes. This introspective study helps you learn from your experience and adapt your approach.

Building a Portfolio of Strategies:

Don't put all your eggs in one basket. Diversify your risk by constructing a portfolio of various trading bots with diverse strategies, asset classes, and risk profiles. This helps balance out volatility and offers stability even if one technique falters.

Remember, diversity is not about flinging spaghetti against the wall and hoping something sticks. Each strategy in your portfolio involves thorough backtesting, risk management, and regular monitoring.

Conclusion: Live trading is both thrilling and nerve-wracking. But with the correct knowledge, planning, and dedication, you can navigate this turbulent terrain and develop your Python bot into a lucrative trading partner. Always remember, that risk management, security, and constant optimization are your partners in this attempt. Go ahead, deploy your bot with confidence, and watch it transform data into riches in the live Forex market arena.

Pro Tip: Consider paper trading your bot before heading into live markets. This gives a secure environment to test your tactics and acquire confidence before risking actual funds.

Part Four : Advanced Topics and Resources

Chapter Ten

Algorithmic Trading Platforms and Tools

As you graduate from building your own Python bot in the sandbox of your development environment, it's time to enter into the actual world of live trading. This step exposes you to algorithmic trading systems, your gateways to implementing your strategy in the dynamic Forex market. This chapter will explore the landscape of major platforms, their essential features, and how to effortlessly connect your Python bot with one to unleash its automated potential.

Popular Algorithmic Trading Platforms:

- MetaTrader 4/5 (MT4/5): A popular and extensively used platform, MT4/5 provides a user-friendly interface, a sophisticated MQL programming language, and access to a vast library of pre-built indicators and expert advisors (EAs). Its popularity draws a wide community of developers and freely accessible materials, making it perfect for beginners and seasoned traders alike.

- NinjaTrader: This platform includes comprehensive charting capabilities, backtesting, and optimization tools, appealing to both visual and technical traders. Its NinjaScript programming language, based on C#, provides versatile coding choices and simplifies interaction with other data sources.

- QuantConnect: A cloud-based platform, QuantConnect reduces the hassle of setting up and maintaining infrastructure, letting you concentrate on strategy formulation and backtesting. Its Python-based Lean Engine accelerates integration for Python fans, and its community-driven library of algorithms gives inspiration and learning possibilities.

- Tradestation: Renowned for its excellent order routing and execution capabilities, Tradestation serves institutional and skilled retail traders. Its proprietary EasyLanguage programming language is strong and adaptable, allowing numerous customization possibilities.

- Interactive Brokers (IB) TWS: A highly complex platform chosen by professionals, IB TWS gives access to worldwide markets, advanced order types, and complete risk management features. Its API permits interaction with several computer languages, including Python, for comprehensive algorithmic control.

Key Features to Consider:

- Supported Programming Languages: Choose a platform compatible with your favorite languages, such as Python, MQL, or C#.
- Backtesting and Optimization Tools: Ensure the platform has powerful

backtesting capabilities to confirm your methods and optimize parameters.

- Live Trading and Order Execution: Choose a platform with a stable connection to your broker and efficient order execution processes.
- Data Feed Access: Select a platform that gives access to the exact Forex data streams you require for your trading techniques.
- Community and assistance: Look for platforms with active user communities and trustworthy technical assistance to help you manage any issues.

Integrating Your Python Bot

- API Libraries: Most platforms provide specific libraries for communicating with your Python bot. These libraries manage communication protocols, authentication, and data exchange between your code and the platform.

- Direct Access: For systems like IB TWS, you can utilize Python libraries like IBpy or IBGPy to achieve direct connection with their API using sockets.

- Wrapper Apps: Some platforms provide wrapper programs that turn your Python code into executable files suitable with their proprietary settings.

- Cloud Integration: Platforms like QuantConnect link easily with cloud-based development environments like Jupyter Notebook, enabling you to write and backtest your Python bot right on their platform.

Remember, Integration specifics and complexity may vary based on your selected platform. Refer to the platform's manual and online resources for particular instructions and examples.

Additional Tips:
- Start with a basic, well-tested Python bot before tackling complicated integrations.
- Focus on knowing the platform's features and tools before going into bespoke integrations.
- Leverage community resources and tutorials to expedite your learning curve.
- Thoroughly test your integration code in a virtual environment before risking real trading.

By equipping yourself with the correct platform and a smooth interface, you unleash the full power of your Python bot and enter boldly into the field of algorithmic Forex trading. Remember, the platform is your launchpad, your Python code the guiding rocket, and thorough testing your fuel for a successful algorithmic trading adventure.

Chapter Eleven

Backtesting and Optimization Techniques

Master the Algorithmic Forge

In the burning furnace of algorithmic trading, where molten code and market data build lucrative strategies, backtesting and optimization rule supreme. They are the expert blacksmiths, refining your trade bots into weapons of accuracy and durability. In this chapter, we dig into the advanced approaches and measurements that enhance your algorithmic advantage, taking you to the promised land of constant earnings.

Advanced Backtesting Methodologies

Gone are the days of rudimentary historical simulations. Modern backtesting leverages complex approaches to give a detailed picture of your strategy's potential:

- Walk-forward optimization: This iterative technique evaluates your strategy on increasingly later data blocks, replicating real-time trading. It avoids "curve-fitting" to prior data, ensuring your technique generalizes effectively to unforeseen market situations.

- Monte Carlo simulations: Imagine numerous virtual marketplaces, each with slightly different settings. Monte Carlo simulations send your plan through this statistical gauntlet, exposing its durability under multiple conditions.

- Sharpe Ratio optimization: This risk-adjusted statistic balances returns against volatility. By optimizing the Sharpe Ratio, you emphasize tactics that generate consistent rewards proportionate to the risk involved.

- Stress testing: Throw everything but the kitchen sink at your strategy! Stress testing exposes it to severe market events like collapses or flash rallies, identifying possible vulnerabilities and improving resilience.

Performance Metrics Beyond the Basics:

The win rate and profit factor are good, but not great. Advanced metrics offer deeper insights:

- Calmar ratio: This measures the maximum drawdown relative to the peak equity, revealing a strategy's ability to weather storms. A higher Calmar ratio indicates better risk management.

- Sortino ratio: Similar to Sharpe Ratio, but penalizes only downside volatility, rewarding strategies that protect profits during losses.

- Maximum drawdown duration: How long does the worst drawdown last? This metric assesses the emotional toll of potential losing streaks.

- Capacity ratio: This measures the maximum capital your strategy can handle before performance deteriorates, helping you scale your bot responsibly.

Optimizing Hyperparameters:

Every strategy has knobs and dials – its hyperparameters. These settings influence its behavior, and finding the perfect combination is key to unlocking its full potential. Optimization techniques like:

- Grid search: Methodically explore all possible combinations of hyperparameter values within a defined range. This exhaustive approach guarantees finding the optimal settings, but can be computationally expensive.

- Genetic algorithms: Mimicking natural selection, this technique iteratively evolves populations of strategies, breeding the best performers to gradually reach peak performance.

- Bayesian optimization: This powerful statistical method identifies promising areas of the hyperparameter space based on previous evaluations, significantly reducing the number of simulations needed.

Refining Your Strategy:

Backtesting and optimization are not one-and-done exercises. They form a continuous feedback loop, constantly refining your strategy:

- Identify weaknesses: Analyze performance metrics and drawdown periods to pinpoint areas for improvement.

- Adapt and evolve: Don't be afraid to adjust your strategy based on market changes and new insights. Remember, the market is a living beast, and your bot should evolve to survive.

- Diversification is key: Don't put all your eggs in one basket. Diversify your portfolio across different strategies and asset classes to mitigate risk and enhance overall returns.

Remember, Backtesting and optimization are powerful tools, but they are not crystal balls. The market is inherently unpredictable, and no strategy can guarantee perfect results. Use these techniques to build robust and adaptable strategies, manage risk effectively, and continuously strive for improvement. With dedication and a relentless pursuit of algorithmic excellence, you can forge your path to a brighter future in the ever-evolving landscape of algorithmic trading.

Beyond the Chapter:

This chapter has provided a glimpse into the advanced world of backtesting and optimization. As you delve deeper, remember these resources:

- Books: "Advances in Financial Machine Learning" by Marcos Lopez de Prado,

"Active Portfolio Management" by Richard Grinold and Ronald Kahn

- Online Courses: QuantConnect, Coursera's "Algorithmic Trading for Everybody" Specialization
- Community Forums: Quantocracy, Reddit's r/algotrading

Embrace the challenge, wield the tools of backtesting and optimization like a master blacksmith, and let your algorithmic creations carve a path to consistent profits in the fiery furnace of the Forex market.

Chapter Twelve

The Future of Algorithmic Trading

As the dust settles on the algorithmic trading revolution, it's clear that the future of this field is as exciting as it is uncertain. New trends and technologies are emerging, reshaping the landscape and promising even greater advancements in automated market interactions. But amidst this technological surge, ethical considerations and responsible trading practices remain paramount.

In this chapter, we delve into both the cutting-edge and the moral compass of algorithmic trading, exploring what lies ahead in this ever-evolving field.

Emerging Trends and Technologies:

- Artificial Intelligence (AI): Machine learning algorithms are already making waves in algorithmic trading, but the future holds even greater potential. Deep learning, reinforcement learning, and natural language processing (NLP) are set to unlock deeper market insights, develop advanced predictive models, and even optimize trading strategies in real time. Imagine bots capable of not only analyzing data but also understanding news sentiment, anticipating policy changes, and even adapting their behavior based on market psychology. This level of intelligent automation is on the horizon.

- Big Data and Data Analytics: The deluge of financial data, from social media feeds to satellite imagery, offers a treasure trove of untapped insights. Advancements in big data processing and analytics will empower traders to extract hidden patterns, predict market movements with greater accuracy, and develop hyper-personalized trading strategies tailored to individual risk profiles and preferences. The line between algorithmic trading and personalized financial guidance will continue to blur as AI and big data converge.

- High-Frequency Trading (HFT) and Quantum Computing: The quest for speed in execution will likely see HFT algorithms reach even lower latencies, leveraging quantum computing capabilities to gain infinitesimal time advantages. However, concerns regarding fairness and market stability will need to be addressed to ensure a level playing field and prevent HFT from exacerbating market volatility.

- Decentralized Finance (DeFi) and Blockchain: The rise of blockchain technology and DeFi platforms opens up new avenues for algorithmic trading. Automated bots can operate within decentralized exchanges, trade tokenized assets, and execute complex investment strategies without relying on traditional intermediaries. While exciting, navigating the regulatory landscape and mitigating security risks will be crucial for widespread adoption in DeFi algorithmic trading.

Ethical Considerations and Responsible Trading Practices:

- Transparency and Explainability: As algorithms become increasingly complex, the need for transparency grows. Traders and regulators alike need to understand how decisions are made by these automated systems. Explainable AI techniques can make algorithms more transparent, allowing users to see why certain trades are executed and fostering trust in the system.

- Algorithmic Bias and Fairness: Algorithmic trading models are susceptible to biases inherent in the data they are trained on. This can lead to discriminatory outcomes, such as perpetuating gender or racial inequalities in access to financial markets. Developers and practitioners must be vigilant in identifying and mitigating algorithmic bias to ensure fair and equitable market participation.

- Market Manipulation and Flash Crashes: The power of high-frequency algorithms poses a risk of market manipulation and flash crashes. Regulatory frameworks and technical safeguards need to be implemented to prevent algorithmic arms races and ensure market stability.

- Human Oversight and Accountability: While automation offers efficiency and precision, human oversight remains crucial. Ethical trading practices require developers and traders to establish clear risk management protocols, set stop-loss orders, and monitor algorithmic operations to prevent excessive losses and unforeseen consequences.

- Education and Knowledge Sharing: As algorithmic trading evolves, it's crucial to democratize knowledge and foster responsible practices. Educational resources, training programs, and open-source software initiatives can empower individuals to participate in algorithmic trading while upholding ethical principles.

Conclusion:

The future of algorithmic trading is a canvas painted with innovation, opportunity, and challenges. New technologies promise powerful tools and unprecedented insights, but ethical considerations and responsible practices must guide our exploration. By prioritizing transparency, fairness, and accountability, we can ensure that algorithmic trading serves as a force for good, democratizing access to financial markets and promoting a more stable and inclusive financial ecosystem.

Remember, the most advanced algorithms are not just lines of code but reflections of the values we imbue in them. As we step into the future of algorithmic trading, let us choose wisely the code we write and the values we encode.

Epilogue

Your Algorithmic Trading Journey

As you've journeyed through this book, you've equipped yourself with the knowledge and tools to embark on an exciting adventure in algorithmic Forex trading. But remember, this is just the beginning. Success in this world requires not just technical prowess, but also dedication, continuous learning, and a healthy dose of perseverance.

Final Tips for Algorithmic Triumph:

- Stay disciplined: Don't let emotions sway your trading decisions. Stick to your backtested strategies, manage risks diligently, and avoid the lure of chasing quick profits.

- Never stop learning: The Forex market is dynamic, and algorithms constantly evolve. Dedicate time to learning new techniques, studying the latest research, and adapting your strategies accordingly.

- Embrace the iterative process: Backtesting, optimization, and refinement are continuous loops. Be prepared to adjust your code, test new ideas, and learn from your mistakes.

- Community is key: Surround yourself with fellow algorithmic traders, mentors, and experts. Discuss challenges, share ideas, and learn from each other's experiences. Joining online forums, attending workshops, or even forming your algorithmic trading group can be invaluable.

- Celebrate the wins, and learn from the losses: Every trade holds a lesson. Take pride in your successes, but analyze your losses objectively to identify areas for improvement. Treat every trade as a stepping stone on your journey towards consistent profitability.

Resources for Continuous Exploration:
- Books: Dive deeper into specific topics with advanced books on algorithmic trading, quantitative finance, and machine learning.

- Blogs and Forums: Stay updated on market trends, new technologies, and

100

community discussions through reputable blogs and online forums dedicated to algorithmic trading.

- Online Courses and Workshops: Numerous online platforms offer comprehensive courses and workshops covering various aspects of algorithmic trading, from coding fundamentals to advanced strategy development.

- Algorithmic Trading Conferences and Events: Attend industry conferences and events to network with professionals, learn from experts, and discover cutting-edge techniques.

Remember, algorithmic trading is not a shortcut to riches. It's a powerful tool that requires knowledge, discipline, and dedication. But for those who persevere, the rewards can be substantial. So, continue learning, refining your skills, and building your algorithmic arsenal. The Forex market awaits your algorithmic prowess. May your trades be profitable, your journey enriching, and your success story an inspiration to others.

Go forth and conquer, algorithmic trader!

Appendix

Common Python Libraries for Algorithmic Trading

- NumPy: Foundational library for numerical computing, array manipulation, and mathematical operations.
- pandas: High-performance data analysis and manipulation library, essential for handling financial dataframes.
- pandas-ta: Specialized library built on top of pandas, offering a wide range of technical indicators for financial analysis.
- TA-Lib: C++ library with Python bindings, providing a comprehensive collection of technical analysis indicators.
- Matplotlib: Powerful plotting library for visualizing financial data, charts, and indicators.

- SciPy: Collection of scientific computing algorithms and functions for optimization, statistics, and more.
- Backtrader: Open-source framework for backtesting trading strategies with a focus on performance and ease of use.
- Zipline: Another popular backtesting library, often used in conjunction with Quantopian's online platform.
- PyAlgoTrade: Event-driven algorithmic trading library for developing and deploying live trading bots.
- Quantopian (API): Online platform for researching and developing trading algorithms, with a Python API for integration.

Glossary of Key Terms and Concepts

- Algorithmic Trading: Automated trading using computer programs to execute strategies based on predefined rules.

- Forex (Foreign Exchange): Global market for exchanging currencies, with high liquidity and trading volume.

- Technical Analysis: Method of analyzing financial markets using past price and volume data to identify patterns and trends.

- Fundamental Analysis: Method of evaluating the intrinsic value of assets based on economic and financial factors.

- Trading Bot: Automated software program that executes trading strategies without human intervention.

- Backtesting: Process of testing a trading strategy on historical data to evaluate its potential performance.
- Paper Trading: Simulating trades without risking real money, used for testing strategies and practicing trading skills.
- Live Trading: Executing trades in the real market with real money, involving risk and potential for profit or loss.
- Risk Management: This crucial aspect of trading involves techniques to control and limit potential losses.
- Position Sizing: Determining the appropriate amount of capital to allocate to each trade, based on risk tolerance and strategy.
- Machine Learning: Application of artificial intelligence to analyze data and

make predictions, increasingly used in algorithmic trading.

Sample Python Code for Basic Trading Strategies

Moving Average Crossover Strategy:

Python
import pandas as pd
# Load historical price data
data = pd.read_csv("fx_data.csv")
# Calculate short-term and long-term moving averages
short_ma

```
= data["Close"].rolling(window=20).mean()
```

```
long_ma
```

```
= data["Close"].rolling(window=50).mean()
```

```
# Generate buy and sell signals
```

```
signals = pd.DataFrame(index=data.index)
```

```
signals["Signal"] = 0.0 # Initialize signals as
neutral
```

```
signals["Signal"] = np.where(short_ma >
```

```
long_ma, 1.0, 0.0) # Buy when short MA
crosses above long MA
```

```
signals["Signal"] = np.where(short_ma <
```

long_ma, -1.0, signals["Signal"]) # Sell when short MA crosses below long MA
... (Implement trading logic based on signals)
Use code with discretion. Learn more

Momentum Strategy:

```python
import pandas as pd


# ... (Load data as above)
# Calculate momentum indicator (e.g., RSI)
rsi = ta.
momentum.RSIIndicator(close=data["Close"], window=14)
```

```
# Generate buy and sell signals based on RSI
thresholds

signals = pd.DataFrame(index=data.index)

signals["Signal"] = 0.0

signals["Signal"] = np.where(rsi < 30, 1.0, 0.0)
#


Buy when RSI is below 30 (oversold)

signals["Signal"] = np.where(rsi > 70, -1.0,

signals["Signal"]) # Sell when RSI is over 70
(overbought)

# ... (Implement trading logic based on signals)

Use code with discretion. Learn more
```

Remember: These are simplified instances for illustration reasons. Real-world trading methods may incorporate more advanced reasoning, risk management, and optimization approaches.